# Whispers of the Muse

## sonnets from magic hill

Philip Boulding

# Dedication

Dedicated in loving memory to my father, Kenneth E. Boulding (1910-1993), and to my mother, Elise Boulding, who continues to encourage and inspire me.

Special thanks to my wife Pam, our sons Geoffrey, Brenin, Morgan, Marshall, their wives, our daughter Brittany, and our five granddaughters, Rowan, Kailey, Lindsey, Margaret and Bridget—for all your love, talents, humor and inspiration.

Special thanks also to Celeste Bennett for all her work with layout and design.

Thanks also to so many friends too numerous to mention. And lastly, to the Muse...even though she abandons me from time-to-time.

*Philip Boulding*

# Contents

## A Universe of Love

**sonnets for love and marriage (continued)**



## The Rising New Matriarchy

**sonnets for the granddaughters**



## Milestones

**sonnets for momentous occasions**

## The Future Isn't What it Used to Be

### sonnets for time and whimsy



## Stories of our Souls

### sonnets for parting, and the journey



## A Yuletide Tradition

### sonnets for the seasons

## A Yuletide Tradition

### sonnets for the seasons [continued]



## Epilogue

# Whispers of the Muse

## sonnets from magic hill

# Introduction

I grew up listening to my father's sonnets. He would write and recite them for special family events; and so it was on the occasion of my parent's 50th wedding anniversary that I set about to compose my first sonnet, to honor them. Thus began my journey of creating poetry to chronicle my family's life, and personal reflections.

My wife and I came from large and loving families, then nurtured one of our own, and a musical one at that. Now four of our five have married, and are creating the next generation; there is no end to inspiration...

Although I love to write poetry, I consider myself a musician first. Over the years my harp music has become linked to the recitation of my sonnets, so the two art forms have come together. The poem sets a stage, and the music then animates it.

Despite the fact that the sonnet form reaches back in time, my father demonstrated its ability to communicate lyrically to the modern ear. In a similar way, the harp does this with music. Both are old yet timeless archetypes that live in the blueprint of the human psyche. They can move the soul to laughter, tears or repose as powerfully today as they did in ancient times.

My father wrote hundreds of sonnets and verse during his life; but he was better known as an economist, scientist, philosopher, and innovative thinker. He was also a humanitarian, Quaker, artist, husband and father of five (I'm number four). He was a renaissance man with a brilliant mind and wit, whom everybody loved, because he loved everyone. Writing sonnets was an activity inspired by his love for Shakespeare's sonnets, and his upbringing in England. For all his own profound body of work, he had a light-hearted manner about him; he often referred to himself as a 'pre-Beatle Liverpudlian'.

As he drew closer to death, his spirit grew brighter, and his sonnet writing became even more prolific. During one of my last visits to Boulder before he died, I read some of my sonnets to him. My father pointed his finger accusingly at me and said "You have stolen my Muse!" Not so. I knew her from his sonnets; she stayed close by his side until the moment of his death. So did my equally illustrious mother, who accepted this 'other mistress' with the most profound grace!

This collection provides something of a glimpse into my family's life—I hope you enjoy it. If you find something that resonates with you, I will be delighted.

*Philip Boulding*

# A Future World to Be

## sonnets for reflection, nature and freedom

# The Journey

My soul is forged upon the anvil of the earth,
Between the coals of hell and heaven's mighty rod.
'Til death I part, and from the moment of my birth,
With joy I take my burden 'cross this dusty sod!
And as I build my fortress, gods will envy me—
Not so to toss my cares upon the fate-less winds—
For I alone among the starry hosts am free,
To ride the waves of destiny with willing wings.
The journey, not the destination, thus I seek;
As slowly truth reveals her solemn, steadfast face,
Until, sufficiently matured, I stand with grace
Upon the Holy Mountain, and my Maker meet!

August 2007

# 'Ohana Kai

## family of the sea

The rolling waves, whose gentle power strive
To pound and hew this island's jagged stone,
With simple and persistent patience, hone
A work of art no mortal could contrive!
The labor of aloha here is done;
And what is left after a work so grand?
A lovely carpet of the finest sand—
—Each grain a testament of All-in-One.
Such wonder, as upon the shore I swoon,
To hear the constant dialogue of sea
And earth and wind and fire calling to me,
Beneath the warming sun and shining moon—
'Tis here the ancient primal lullaby
Sings to my soul with its eternal sigh!

February 2006
Maui

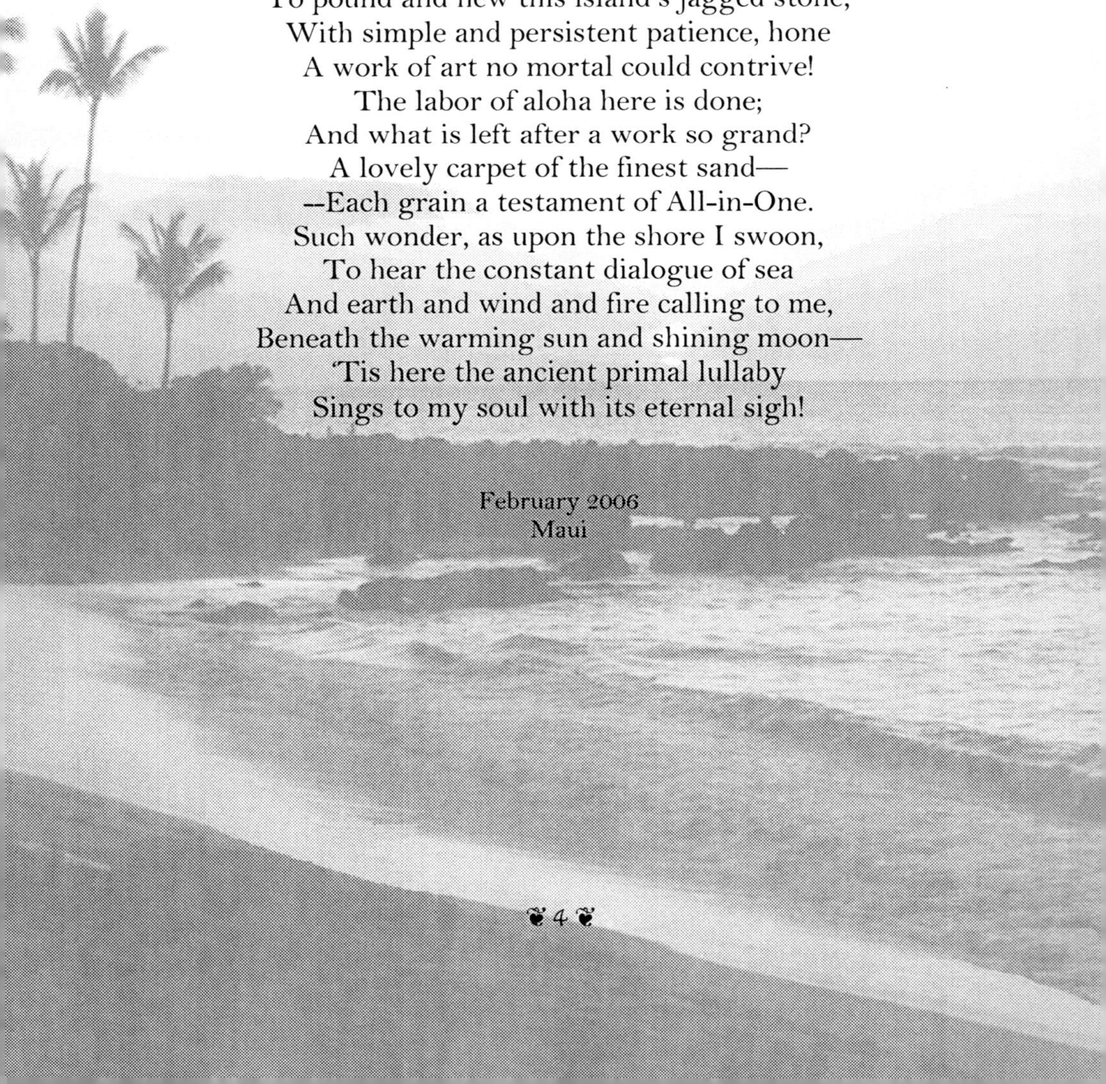

# Holy Island

O' ancient melody! Whence comest thou –
I hear thy echo in the stillness of this holy place.
O' mothering island of saints and pilgrims –
The blood from the wounds of the world
Waters thy sacred ground
As garden for soul's flowering.

O' Holy Island, as thou riseth above the lapping waters
With the countenance of noble individuality,
So shall we arise from all earth's trials,
Strengthened by the King of the Elements
Whose touch did cause the very heart of the earth
To tremble, and rejoice!

Legends of antiquity etched upon thy stone
Speak of the forces of light and dark that shaped thee.
Thy tower stands as guardian over time that was, is,
and shall be –
Man transformed, as spheres of future harmony!

# The Bard's Advice to the King

O' people, hearken! 'Twas in times of old,
The Bard his tales would tell, and songs would sing,
To raise the spirit of both thrall and king;
Heed now his words, if wisdom there be told:
O' King of this great land o'er all the earth,
With power to destroy her in your hands
She trembles, at your thundering commands
For war, while peace she yearns to bring to birth!
If peace is good, and war is evil, pray,
Consider reconciliation's task—
'Tis what all seekers after truth would ask—
That wisdom be our guide, and love hold sway.
The Light that shines on darkness, like the sun,
Illumines all humanity as one!

December 2002

# Where Dragons Dance

The Bards of ancient times sought to espouse
The mystical three moods, meant to arouse
First joy, and then deep sorrow; thus repose—
Yet how about a fourth? One might propose
Bewilderment! --for these perplexing times,
To guide us through the contradicting lines
Of paradox; of love, and peace, and hate,
And war, and conflict driving mankind's fate...
If Muses could but seek to part the veil
Of hidden worlds, that shroud the serpent's tail
Entwined in every striving human heart,
Then love's redeeming power might impart
A vision of a future world to be,
Where dragons dance, and all is harmony!

November 2001

# The Dragon Harp

With serpent branch I beckoned unto thee—
By nature's wild unbeaten path I came,
Awaiting you to make a harp of me—
Let it be known, that Wormwood is my name!

I trod the earth unseen by human toil--
Though beastly countenance must be my lot,
Yet flowers bloom from my unworthy soil
Without which shining beauty would be nought.

So sound forth now, my pulsing steely strings—
O' bardic hands, draw forth my fiery breath,
To mediate the trials of birth and death,
And lift the lowly to the thrones of Kings!

Redemption from the darkness you will bring,
When, with the voice of angels, dragons sing!

July, 2007

# Sonnet for Reconciliation

Few dare believe the words of He who said:
"Now walk the extra mile, and turn the cheek –
Yes, love your enemy, forgive the bleak
And weary ways of humankind's great dread!"
If true compassion nurtured anger's soil
Then deserts would miraculously bloom
And bring new light to mankind's endless gloom–
A hope of all wars end, by love's great toil.
Yet are these words of dreamers' starry eyes?
Or visions to transform our world anew?
What else? Must we then turn ourselves into
The likeness of that which we would despise?
It is of life a troubling mystery,
That love must conquer hate relentlessly.

(following 9-11-2001)

# Hymn to the Morning

Thou soul
Be silent
As the Angel wakes thee
With the morning sun
Thy thoughts run
Like the furies
of the wind –
Let thy spirit still them
And be renewed in thy thinking
Though passions roar
Like a raging river
Let thy Guardian take hold of them
And bring you the word of peace,
All abiding and eternal

The Guardian shall transform
Thy loneliness
Into Love
That embraces All Things
Into Wisdom
That knows All Things

And thus into humility,
That thy desire is transformed
To the depth of Will
To serve All Things
From the lowest to the highest

July 14, 2001
Magic Hill Hermitage

# Sonnet for Community

Community is something hard to find
Though everywhere on earth it can be seen
It lives not in a place, but state of mind
Where, hearts and wills enjoined, a greater being
Is thus created, nurtured by ideals
Born of that which each person thinks and feels.
Though life become a daily drudgery
Do stop and look about from time to time
We have each other, that is plain to see
But looking deeper, see the vast gold mine
Of wisdom, love, in parent, teacher, child.
For what nobler task might we undertake,
That lower forces strive we to refine,
And in each other fan the flame Divine?

April 4, 1993
Morning Star Waldorf School

# A Universe of Love

sonnets for love and marriage

# Sonnet for My Mother and Father

## celebrating fifty years of marriage

Ere I came, as spirit hov'ring o'er earth
I must have thought my time had come to learn
Of the enduring fires of love that burn;
For you I chose as blessing for my birth!

As human love does fail and marriages fall,
You stand as mighty beacons for us all,
For in your presence frozen hearts would thaw,
And by your steadfast love we stand in awe.

Yes, even in my name is love's name found.
By light of love my life is ever bound
To one who shares life's deepest mysteries.
To what great secret do I hold the keys?

By fire of passion we can be consumed...
By fire of spirit we can be transformed!

Summer 1990❦

❦This was my first sonnet, written en-route to
Boulder, Colorado,
for a family celebration.

# Sonnet to Calm the Storms

## advice to the groom and bride

If e'r with woman in a tempest caught,
And find a temper flared, think on this thought:

A greater love hath no woman than she
Who chastises a man for his own sake;
And greater love would have no man than he
Who listens, and with inner calm does make
From storms, a place of refuge for the soul—
A dwelling wherein peace can make them whole.

Now just in case you think I'm pre-disposed
To think of man and woman thusly posed,
(For in this "liberated" fray we're fraught
With statements and rebuttals come to naught!)
Know that, although these statements seem adverse,
The same applies if stated in reverse!

June 14, 1994

# Sonnet for Geoffrey and Erin's Wedding

One could approach a wedding with a mind
For mathematics, if one felt inclined
But love, for numbers, really doesn't care
Yet for dramatics, seems to have a flair –

From graduation straight to wedded bliss
The fullness of life's lessons you'll not miss
I wonder if I might have some advice
For this pair so well suited and "un-viced":

True love dwells joyously in mutual passion,
But pleasure one must dutifully ration
For noble love is rare and precious-found
When each for the other are freedom-bound.

When all the fuss is finally said and done,
What's left is gold, when one plus one makes…one!

June 14, 1994

# Sonnet for Brenin and Sara's Wedding

What solemness and joy we juxtapose
As we anticipate these wedding vows
Which stirring words shall deep in us arouse
A sense of noble union of two souls.

A courtship long and slow was their design,
And not that certainty was e'er at stake
Nor depth of their devotion could one shake
Yet love, as patience, waited for its sign.

As in all marriage, more than two are wed,
But in this case we've gotten quite a spread!
May love's intent so fill their world and shine
Through all the trials, and all the tests of time.

Let's toast to love, and hold up high our glasses
For lots of little red-haired lads and lasses!

March 26, 1999

# Sonnet for Marshall and Abby's Wedding

Four generations gather to rejoice
And celebrate this solemn wedding vow—
And so, upon reflection, please allow
Me to congratulate you on your splendid choice!

My father once to marriage gave this key,
He termed it thus: "put-up-ability".
Now on one level this, mundane, might sound
But holy grace is built on humble ground.

In marriage we accept both gift and task
Of love, to serve and freely build upon
The lure of sweet romance, which leads us on
To higher paths concealed behind its mask.

May happiness be yours as you aspire
Together in love's true transforming fire!

September 16, 2000

# Sonnet for Morgan and Lara's Wedding

Upon this curved and rock-strewn path of life,
As though within a maze we twist and wind,
Until, with certain lessons learned, we find
An answer to our questing heart's long strife:

Another soul who shines with our own light,
And in each-other's hearts, perhaps reflect
The truth of spirit that none can deflect,
And so we celebrate the end of night!

The mystery of marriage lies in this:
That, though two souls unite beyond their sum,
And ever growing, yet become more one—
Thus they, respecting freedom in their bliss,
Create, and procreate, and then above
All else, transform our universe to love!

September 7, 2000

# Sonnet for Carew and Aaron's Wedding

A sense of solemn and auspicious fare
Does seem to permeate this mountain air.
Indeed, Carew and Aaron have a flare
For meeting in high places rich and rare...

Perhaps a higher calling summons these
Two souls with whom we celebrate this day.
Integrity and Purpose light their way
Inspired by love; so may this wedding please
The Lord's intent for merging of two beings:
To represent our strivings' furthest aim,
To learn to live in harmony, and tame
This wounded world's old passions, 'til truth rings.

Together may you seek vistas sublime
With each new mountain peak you face and climb!

Grand Lake Lodge, Colorado
August 31, 2002

# Sonnet for Priscilla and Jim's Wedding

What joyous spirit fills this gathering place,
As families meld with families and rejoice,
And celebrate our gladness with one voice
Priscilla's and Jim's union, full of grace.

Amidst God's greatest splendor, where they dwell
Within the Master Landscaper's great care –
The secrets of their souls reveal and share
A destiny-filled story yet to tell…

For when two souls unite beyond their sum
These individualities confound
All logic – mathematics can't expound
The reasoning of the heart, where two means one.

And all the world's great minds can't help but feel,
'Tis logic of the heart, this world will heal.

High Mountains of Western Colorado
July 12, 2003

# Sonnet for Katherine and Dino's Wedding

At certain points of time, a timeless realm
Reveals itself, a vision—a surprise!—
—Of all delights eternal, in the guise
Of ordinariness—yet at the helm
Stands One all-knowing as for time and place,
When marriage shall bestow it's profound grace.
In this we are the teacher and the taught
Embarking on a pilgrimage of light,
No strangers to the walk that tries soul's might,
No lessons learned with battles left un-fought.
Yet will and intellectual power pales
Without the life and pulse that love regales
Upon us human curiosities—
It is indeed the crown of mysteries!

# Sonnet for My Valentine

I sit with pen in hand, and wait for words
To flow from heart and mind, like songs of birds
Or fragrant blossoms wafting on the breeze
But words of worthy weight won't come with ease!
Our love has grown beyond that simple place –
And poets, mute, accept with humble grace
A realm beyond, which words cannot describe
But only tarry near to love's sweet bribe
Of sensual delights (which we'll not shun!)
Yet oceans to explore we've just begun

Though for eternity we've danced as one
It seems as though our journey's never done –
You are the sail, and I the anchor free –
Uncharted and unbounded is our sea!

February 14, 1999

# I Awoke to See My Lady Fair

I awoke to see my lady fair
With blazing hair
Just lying there
So unaware
That in my gazing
Upon her blazing
Countenance, though dreaming
Thoughts near spiritual came they streaming—
That I love this woman
With all my heart,
With all my body, mind and soul—

And yet, with all this loving being such,
I wish, O' God, that I loved thee as much!

New Year's Day, 1994

# The Rising New Matriarchy

## sonnets for the granddaughters

# Sonnet for Rowan

## on her first birthday

You, blessed child, from realms of glory came.
Before your entrance, "sailboat" was your name,
As if on cosmic seas you sailed and flew
With destiny's great call, to those you knew.

With searching eyes and solemn countenance,
You find a world both beautiful and tense --
Yet when you smile, the landscape lights ablaze,
And we just bask within your joyous gaze!

When ere I look into your eyes I see
A window to the wondrous world you left
To be with us – O' how we welcome thee!
And how the spirit-world must feel bereft!

Grow like the tree, O' Rowan, stalwart one –
With roots in earth, and branches to the Sun!

April 11, 2001

# Sonnet for Kailey

## on her first birthday

So rarely in this life have I yet seen
A child with such a joyous, radiant sheen
For her a smile will calm the wildest storm,
And part the darkest clouds in cold of night
Then bringing forth the sun to make us warm
She showers us with laughter's sweet delight.

But that which most endears this child to me
And may indeed become her golden key
Is what she gives in upward reaching arms,
While loosing every hold upon my love –
A gesture that so totally disarms –
And leaves my soul defenseless as a dove!

May Kailey's light so melt this world's old wrath
That every heart will brighten in her path!

June 2001

# Margaret's Arrival

She came to earth in chariots of gold
And trailing clouds of star-dust; angel's song
Accompanied as thunder pealed along,
But no one heard or saw, like tales of old…
We waited quietly right here on earth,
With our own trails of glory long-forgot—
Such is the human struggle and our lot—
Thus baited breath awaits each coming birth.

She came in silence, and I saw those eyes;
Like water, fathomless deep pools of peace;
Like sunlight, warming with it's shining love;
Like earth, with all it's wonder, wherein lies
A path for thee; thus may you boldly stride,
And 'midst the world's old sorrows, turn the tide!

November 23, 2003

# Sonnet for Lindsey

Dear Lindsey, from the day that you were born,
The brightness of your spirit filled each place,
With joy and laughter, and upon your face
A smile was never absent; did adorn
Each nook and edifice that you explored
As up and down you went, and in and out
Where only infant curiosity could route—
As we looked on in wonder, and adored
This youth—where did she come from? Happiness
Does seem to be her lot, and nothing less—
And so, what might we learn from this sweet child,
Whose temperament does woo us, bold yet mild?
I do not know, but this I will now say,
That where 'er she goes, she turns the night to day!

November 2007

# Sonnet for Bridget

Rejoice! For unto us a child is born
Into this world of strife and sorrow, ripe
With need for harvest—hark! An archetype
Which hearkens back to that first Christmas morn!

With eyes that shine bright as the morning star,
We gaze in humble reverence at this gift
From heaven, which the angels bring to lift
Our soul's remembrance, whence we came, afar...

O' Bridget! Bride of light! May you enfold
The One who held the King upon her breast,
And gave to God born unto earth sweet rest
For this, the world's new upward rising soul
And mind and heart and spirit winging free
Amidst the tumult, to eternity!

November 2006

# Milestones

## sonnets for momentous occasions

# A Toast to Brittany

## carnegie hall

Here's to our lovely daughter Brittany
Who walks with poise upon the grandest stage
And with such grace does artfully engage
An orchestra's celestial harmony.

Now that you have debuted Carnegie Hall
(And that, before your parents, after all!)
The world is easily within your reach,
But hold it gently, heal it, let it teach.

The gift of music must flow selflessly –
Yet that you've known since such a little child
Its magic comes from realms unknown and wild;
Inspires us to states of ecstasy.

So as your destiny becomes unfurled
May music from your hands so bless this world!

May 7, 2000

# Sonnet for Brittany's Graduation

## rice university

What is the cause of celebration here –
Is it not the most joyous day this year?
Nay, 'tis the happiest of twenty years plus one,
Since angels' fanfare first announced "She's come! –
To earth, a gift of music rare and wild,
A beauteous soul of wisdom, yet a child."

Upon four years of nurturing at Rice,
A Goldsmith[1] here has fashioned something nice
To stoke the brightest flames of Colburn's[2] fire,
Where precious metals, tempered, dreams aspire!

With Lipsett[3] firm, and future glowing bright
A chapter comes to closure on this night.
Though parents, proud, are beaming like the stars,
The World will claim her, saying, "She is ours!"

May 8, 2004

[1]Professor Kenneth Goldsmith welcomed Brittany into his violin studio at Rice University's Shepherd School of Music four years ago.

[2]Brittany was offered a full fellowship for graduate studies with Robert Lipsett at the Colburn School of Performing Arts in Los Angeles.

[3]Robert Lipsett is one of the most sought after violin professors in the country.

# Sonnet for Professor Goldsmith

I would not trade for all of China's teas
That one great treasure beyond all compare—
The priceless pearl? No, something far more rare—
For which we thank you on our bended knees!

'Tis true, the stuff of clay and genius
Is God's domain, and given to our keep—
Yet how we guide, that destiny may reap
The spirit's riches from that soil, and trust
To rise from out the cosmic forge this dust
Transformed to gold through all your labors thus:
Behold—a shining star is born to represent
The music of the spheres, from whence we came—
One Brittany, our daughter, is her name—
And you, the Goldsmith, rightly stake her claim!

May 8, 2004

# Sonnet for Hospitality

How can one measure gratitude when faced
With friends who know no bounds at all
For their good kindness to both kings and thrall,
Yet everything they do is fully graced
With generosity beyond compare?
To this, I must admit, I do not dare
To look at scales, or see the balance weights
Which doubtless find me wanting at the gates
Of judgment—yet, who judges when it's love
From God's great bounty given from above?
We thus most humbly give our gratitude
To those whose hearts reflect God's attitude
Of giving long before one's self relaxes—
Especially through hearts as big as Texas!

May 16, 2004
Houston, Texas

# Sonnet for Morgan's Graduation

## wheaton college

This is a celebration most sublime
A milestone in your path upon the earth
A place to see ahead and look behind,
And set new sights on vistas of great worth.

You've worked admirably hard to get this far;
And you've filled your mind with physics galore –
Yet don't forget, in life there's so much more –
See failure and success for what they are.

The highest knowledge that one can attain
Serves others, never bought for one's own gain
Thus access to worlds wondrous never end –
May your life's passion toward this goal extend;

So as we celebrate a task well done,
Let's toast to journeys ended and begun!

May 22, 1999
Wheaton College
Norton, MA

# Sonnet for My Mother at 80

## - a toast -

What fullness life has brought your Viking blood!
Just look at all these children gathered here
To celebrate your life from far and near.
At eighty years, you're looking mighty good!

How shall we praise this Matriarch of Peace
When recognition in abundance finds
A humble soul amongst world's greatest minds?
--By loving all we meet with purest grace.

Here's to our stalwart Nordic heritage,
And blessings on this gathering of kin,
Who eighty years from now shall carry on
The work of peace, begun by dear old Mom.

So when comes time to lay thee down to rest,
May heaven's angels grant thee... "**all the best!**"

July 28, 2000
Family Reunion in Leavenworth, Washington
Sleeping Lady

# Sonnet for My Mother's 85th Birthday*

## for elise boulding

You've made it all the way to eighty-five,
And I, for one, am glad you're still alive!
Before too long you'll cross the Great Divide—
For those like you, the doors will open wide,
And vistas un-imagined you will see
As worldly burdens fall and you fly free—
I watch with you, and pray I will not sleep,
As you approach this door to heaven's keep;
And when you enter, would that you may see
A place prepared, near you and Dad, for me.
But please, before you go, do tell us how
You finally learned in life to 'Be Here Now'!

July 6, 2005

*In response to Mom's poem she wrote for her birthday:

"I'm eighty-five and still alive!
What am I called to do?
Get behind the plow?
No, just learn to Be Here Now."

# Sonnet for Mom at 87

'Twas eighty-seven revolutions hence—
(Referring to the earth around the orb)
A light was born upon a distant fjord,
And all in heaven did rejoice at once!

This light grew brighter through the grace of years;
Made peace, and children, (of which I am one)—
Wrote books, and taught her wisdom, and then some—
And gave her gifts with love through wars and tears.

I know this world met not your goals, it seemed—
But visionaries are ahead of time;
The seeds you plant are part of a great vine—
A future world of peace will grow as dreamed!

So don't stop dreaming, 'er at eighty seven—
We'll carry on with you, from here to heaven!

July 6, 2007

# Sonnet for the Architect's Son

A gift more rare than gold you've given here,
In this, your life's great work, a job well done!
A hearty toast to the architect's son.
Words fail a proper eloquence, I fear…
But what is this new gift of which I speak?
A subtle light unveiled before our eyes,
Our souls, wherein the human story lies –
A long and winding journey, sometimes bleak –

This light comes shining through these monuments
Of genius that stand the test of time
Through human folly, yet a love sublime
Reveals our common roots as testaments
Of universal brotherhood – I see,
Indeed, that we are one vast family!

May 24, 2003

# Sonnet for a Birthday

We celebrate a milestone on this day—
—Six decades—and yet numbers come to nought
To such a timeless soul as yours—and ought
We not praise timelessness without delay?

You came from realms of beauty which you poured
Upon this world, regardless of the cost—
Your gifts of love and wisdom are not lost
By those of us so graced by your accord.

If 'er I gave all for one precious pearl,
'Twas destiny, to bring you by my side
And make of love sweet music through the tide
Of life, with scrolls yet to unfurl—

So worlds may come and go, but you, my love,
Will shine with light eternal from above!

October 2006

# Morning in the Garden of the World

It is morning in the garden of the world,
And solitude in paradise is hardly lonely –
Brilliant Sun streams over Tree Cathedrals,
Over lazily waving pastures of daisies
and grasses breezing, buttercups blazing –
Over hummingbirds weaving and songbirds singing
Behind my thoughts drifting three thousand
Miles away to my love…and my mother,
Who birthed me this day, forty-six years ago –
A blink in God's eye (and maybe a wink?)
Yet I don't feel that old, when the world is so new
But I wish, yet I know,
That I share this sweet moment
With you.

July 13, 1999

# The Future Isn't What It Used to Be

sonnets for time and whimsy

# The Future Isn't What It Used To Be

The Future isn't what it used to be—
Nay, never is, nor was, because, you see,
It doesn't run a line so straight to there
From here—the future now is everywhere!
In every moment that we think or scheme,
Or feel, imagine, will or craft or dream,
The future we've created in the now
And unbeknownst to us, or knowing how
The present comes to haunt us from the past,
Unless, with good intentions, we hold fast
The deeds that come full circle to remind—
Us of the debts we must repay in kind!
May That which Was, Is, and ever shall Be
Teach us "Eternal Now-ness" presently…!

# Sonnet for Time

How is it that we humans fuss and whine
About our busy lives and lack of time
When nature hasn't seemed to change her course
(Except where business usurps her resource)?

While with great difficulty we surmise
The quirky ways of men, the sun will rise
and set, and shine its living light on all
Through winter, spring and summer, even fall.

In truth, we have all time at our command—
Eternity created us a place
To work within the web of time and space—
(Though deadlines we best meet for schemes so grand...)

And when we cross to that great "by and by"
We'll ever wonder how the time did fly!

# Ode to My Favorite Shirt

It's over the hill,
A worn out done-deal,
It's grist for the mill,
For worms a good meal.

Alas, in this shirt
I worked hard and played.
It made me look better
Than bare skin betrayed!

For you, dear old friend,
I will shed a quick tear—
But not tarry long,
For indulgence I fear

Is what made me cherish
You so from the start—
True raiment must always
Shine forth from the heart!

So like winter's gloom
Brought to life by the spring,
The cotton fields' bloom
Will another shirt bring!

March 28, 2001

# How I Almost Brought About the End of the World

My Muse and I, to be quite clear,
Were in a tiff one day;
I'd too much to do, and places to go
As I entered the Yuletide fray.

An then, at one point, said I to her,
(As this project made my hair curl)
"Honestly, Muse, if it doesn't get done,
It won't be the end of the world."

"Yes, it will!" said she, with considerable force,
and that most emphatically –
To which, I dropped my pen, and thought,
To myself, "Whoa – could it be?"

And then my thoughts, being such as they are,
To run so wild began,
"If I don't get this project done,
T'will be the end of Man!"

Imagination shook free of its reigns,
As I pondered the ramification
Of how a mere act of omission by me,
Could cause such world-wide devastation!

So craftily my mind did work,
With all my new-found power—
My letters to the leaders of the world
Will make them cower!

I'll halt every war, and stop global warming;
And health care and schools will be free –
Enlightenment will be the call of the day
And all, because of me!

Just then, the phone rang, and brought me to earth
In such a remarkable way –
I smiled, grabbed my pen, put my hand to the plow –
And with joy, re-entered the day.

November 14, 2007

# First Touch of Spring

I awaken, and the world feels old and new…
The creative spark within me tingles, a-waiting with childlike joy
To be called into action—
Like the cats, peering wide-eyed through the window at me
With anticipation of their morning meal.
I leap out of bed, and groan with a pollen-drenched sneeze and itchy eyes,
Compliments of the alder forest behind the house by Magic Hill—
Suddenly finches wing to the window, wondering why
There is no finch food in the feeder—
I throw the windows wide, and snatching the feeders, call out:
"Don't go away boys, I'll be right back!"
I return shortly with feeders full, calling out to the hummingbirds,
"Fresh cold drinks, on the house, all around!"
I wonder at how nature continues to rejoice,
In spite of the burdens and suffering we humans have imposed upon her…
And yet the birds sing, to express nature's irrepressible joy…
I sing, because I am free—
I dance, because my body can hardly contain itself, even though it is aging…
I know it will die someday, and I will reluctantly give this precious gift
Back to nature, back to the dust from whence it came,
That it may help future flowers to grow.
I know also, even deep in my hardened bones,
That I will live on after they perish,
Enriched by this brief worldly sojourn.

I will continue to sing, because I am free,
And I will sing this song for you,
And for all the world's suffering,
And for all who think they are lost—
We are not really lost—
We are merely hindered by the lack of directions,
To take us where we know we need to go…
We can ultimately only find them within ourselves—
And because of our freedom (in spite of all our shackles)
This task has been made almost impossible—
And yet, the beauty of the Divine, is that all things are possible—
And in the eyes of the Divine, all things exist—
And therefore, "All that exists is possible"…
This phrase from my father has resonated through the years with me,
Slowly unveiling its mysteries
beneath the mask of absurdity…
He died on this day, fourteen years ago, on the night of St. Patrick's Day.
I feel that he is speaking to me now—
And to him, and to my mother who yet resides with grace upon this earth,
I would say: Thank you—thank you for seeing the possible in me,
Even when I was impossible—
For you gave me the possibility to build a solid spiritual foundation
Upon which I could stand and gaze upon the world—
And create freely within it—
And though one day it may crumble all around me,
Yet my joy abounds in being free.

March 18, 2007
Magic Hill

# The Dishwasher's Ode to the Cook

Though heat of inspiration makes food fly,
Yet mine is not to ask the reason why--
For all the meals with which our home you bless,
The task of cleaning is quite worth the mess!

'Tis privilege and honor most sublime
To rid the world of filth and grease and grime!
So, let the flour spill upon the floor,
(and I'll just quietly sweep it out the door...)

And let the beet juice o'er the counter rain –
I'll figure out a way to mop the stain.
Unlike so many other chores in life,
There is a start and ending to this strife!

All hail to those who really love to cook –
For we who don't, they let us off the hook!

April 11, 2001

# A Question of Self-Healing

## in the mood of dr. seuss

The healing profession is something quite queer—
Assumptions are made, that we somehow hold dear—

"You can't heal yourself—a professional see!"
But I find, the very best healer is me!

To bugs, germs and viruses, their wrath fulfilling,
I put up my dukes— and they see I'm unwilling!

For heaven's sake, stop buying vitamin C—
Get sleep, eat your veggies, and healthy you'll be!

If something starts aching, or hurting inside,
Just visualize light, and you might be surprised!

I'm not against doctors, or surgeons or quacks—
We need the bone-menders, to fill in the gaps…

Some doctors won't like me, if this I be preaching;
But they need not worry, for this I'm not teaching…

It cannot be taught – should I be distraught?
At times I think yes, sometimes I think not!

November 2007

# Stories of our Souls

## sonnets for parting, and the journey

# Sonnet of Farewell

Together in our sojourn here we weave
The stories of our souls we all must tell,
And bonds of brotherhood, before we leave,
Will hold us long ere we've said our farewell.

And in the wide expanses of the world—
Yea, even in the cosmos' starry height—
The daylight of creation first unfurled,
Then rent itself asunder in the night.

So as we journey forth across this earth,
And see that all that lives must also die;
Yet dying, give it's impetus to birth
Of spirit, born of love, and loving strive
To find, in every tearful song's goodbye,
The seeds of greeting, yet to draw us nigh!

March 18, 1993
Written upon hearing of my father's death

# Sonnet to My Father

## #1

Little did I know how well you knew me
During those desolate years of my life.
Which lessons have awakened in my soul
A reverence, a glint, a wonder for that
Which we narrowly perceive as life here,
And for a greater life beyond the veil.

The play of light and darkness holds itself
Uniquely perceived in your mind – because
Of who you are – because of who I am,
Soon will shadows fall away from our eyes.

I give thanks and praise for my pain and strife
For this I think I can say I've learned;
The thorns that cause the battles scars of life
Are stems of roses, e'er blooming, well earned!

January 1993

# Sonnet to My Father
## #2

Now I hold your precious life in my hands
Guiding your wheelchair along Boulder Creek
Even now in the sunset of your days
Each blessed moment holds something fresh for you.

A young couple passes with their stroller
"How nice to have wheels at both ends of life!"
You say with a smile, and your wife replies;
"And to have the roles reversed is quite nice!"

Now a sixteenth grandchild you have acquired –
Another stroller in the wheel of life.
A life well lived you've added to this wheel –
A wealth of spirit you have given us.

First you pushed us, now we are pushing you –
May our lives be as full when we are through!

January 16, 1993
Boulder, Colorado

# Evening Verse for an Earthly Angel

To one who serves as guardian to earth's children –
May the child-like spirit of God surround thee,
Love as vast as the sky enfold thee
Peace as mighty rivers flow about thee
A verdant meadow be thy bed
A starry canopy above thy head
From thy heart all fears fled
From thy body, released all dread
Christ in the starry heavens surround you

With love unending –

Love that knows no heights or depths,
But reaches across the distances, enfolding you
And holding you very, very near.

February 27, 1993
(Written during my last visit with my father before his passing.)

# Sonnet for
# My Father's Parting

Farewell, my father, on this new journey –
So many travels found you at the helm
Which, young, I often feared for your return.
Now that your soul has fled to glorious realms,
I need not fear, but only say "rejoice!"
Nor grieve, not for the loss of your great life
Which, living still, must now fill every voice
With joyful tidings, songs of love, not strife . . .

Yet my heart aches to grasp your loving hand,
To gaze once more upon your countenance
Oh, let me burden you not with sorrow
But freely feel the blessing of your presence . . .

Why flow our tears, as you go to meet your King?
While earth-bound we, you fly on angels wings!

March 24, 1993

# Sonnet to Comfort My Mother's Loss

O' how can I console your emptiness
For the loss of your life-long companion?
No ordinary man—a true champion—
And no one knew him better, nonetheless...

I wish there was a bridge that I could make
From here unto the realm of the beyond,
To step from tempest to a quiet pond...
That land of blessed spirits where he wakes.

What do you think that he is doing there,
Now that no body shackles him to earth?
Writing sonnets to the heavenly spheres,
To shower us with blessings of his mirth!?

A man of peace in life, now he is free—
Go visit him—he holds the door for thee!

April 1993

# Lament for All the World's Deceased

The light of blessing ever must we shine
Upon all soul's deceased, now living free
To contemplate this weary world and see
The complex weaving ways of the Divine.

As nations clash with nations and lament
Their fallen heroes, and their loved ones lost,
How shall we justify this solemn cost
Of lives cast out by further war's foment?

If cast aside we must this mortal frame,
Is't nobler for the spirit if it be
Through acts of peace, not war, thus setting free
The soul's impassioned furies, there to tame?

Alas—with circle broken, we surmise
The forming of a spiral—Earth, arise!

November 2002

# Farewell to Faraway

I sat on time worn steps, over the Bay,
And said farewell to thee in still of night,
With full moon beaming from thy star-filled height,
And now farewell I bid by light of day.

As heav'nly messenger comes and tips its wing—
A hail to mighty heroes of your past,
Whose presence lives with us—though hearts downcast,
We raise our heads and to the future sing!

Four solemn ladies meet to choose your fate
(Whose chemistry mingles in complex ways)
One decides she, stewardship will take
And all to peace with Faraway shall make.

For something greater lives than just a place—
Thy timeless spirit touches us with grace!

June 23, 1994
"Faraway"
Lincolnville Beach, Maine

# A Yuletide Tradition

sonnets for the seasons

# Seasons of the Soul

Our soul is born in light of Spring
And with it inspiration brings
To force of life our task renewed,
That earth with love shall be imbued.

We cross then into Summer fields.
Intoxicating nature wields
Her lure as dreaming soul takes flight
Take care we must to keep our sight.

Matured by Autumn's toil and strife
Then comes courage to face our life
And looking toward the needs of man
Extend we will our helping hand.

When comes the dark of Winter's night
We must kindle an inward light
As the gift of heaven draws near
That love's still voice we all may hear.

Then like a resurrection bring
To earth a new and joyous Spring!

December 1993

# A Solstice Welcome

Dear friends, come gather 'round this Solstice time,
And lay your burdens at the gate sublime,
Where crossing, we shall enter realms above,
And drink the fount of Light's renewing love.

Like seeds of summer planted in earth's fold,
The soul reflects in winter's slumb'ring cold,
The birth of Spirit-Sun 'midst worldly ways,
Which heralds now the lengthening of days!

Upon returning to this earthly round,
And magic in the ordinary found,
This light will shine toward all whom we may meet,
And bring the higher nature forth to greet.

These soul-seeds then will burst forth in the spring
'Midst nature's joyous re-awakening!

2002

# The Bard's Welcome

Dear friends, come gather 'round this Yuletide night,
To celebrate with joy, the coming light—
In this, the darkest hour of the year,
While nature sleeps and angels hover near.

With spirits bright we'll fan the fire of love
That overcomes all discord, like the dove
Who brings the cherished olive branch of peace
And hope in reconciliation's grace.
The highest challenge of our human race—
To nurture all, the greatest and the least!

The walls of paradise are built of stone
Which contradictions left and right condone—
Yet child-like through the gates we'll walk, in time,
To stand forth free, and let our souls' light shine!

2004

## Beneath a Star

Come O' travel-weary kings and shepherds,
Meet thou at the crossroads of time.
Beneath a star a radiant child of promise
Spreads peace o'er all the earth
Rejoice and celebrate now His birth!

1994

## Bridge of Light

Come light a fire in the hearth,
And on this cold and wintry eve,
Open the door to all who knock;
The Bard with song shall greet thee:

"Bring goodwill to brave the dark
For Noble Love is born this night,
To reconcile all human hearts
And lead us to the Bridge of Light!"

1996

## Yuletide Welcome

We welcome all this Yuletide eve!
May joy be yours, and 'ere we leave,
With mirth we'll celebrate the light
That shines in midst of winter's night.

So open wide your heart and mind—
Let truth be sought, and therein find
A spark to kindle from above,
And blazing, give to all our love!

1984

## Mummer's Verse

Mummers, Mimers, Dreamers & Rhymers!
Come thou hence and lift our minds
And hearts above the daily grinds
Of life, and strife, and worldly woes!
A joyful dance or song compose –
Not one of peace, or sweet repose –
But laughter, mirth, bring to us here,
To carry us lightly through the year!

December 16, 1994

# Earth's Deep Dark Long Night

It was on Earth's deep, dark, long night—
There came a lantern bright,
That left er' sorrow bade it part
A light in every heart,
A light in every heart…

When came the fullness of the day
He danced on land and sea
Another's hand did send Him forth
To teach and set us free,
To teach and set us free…

And when came time for Sun's mid-stride,
He fought the dragon fierce.
With all the power of His love,
The heart of darkness pierced,
The heart of darkness pierced…

Then came the greatest feat of all,
'Twas in the light of spring.
He gave His body to the earth,
And spirit rose up singing,
And spirit rose up singing…

It was on Earth's deep, dark, long night—
There came a lantern bright…

Song written for Celtic Yuletide 1998

# Epilogue

# Apology to the Muse

She whispers gently in my ear
Such words I often yearn to hear—
And then again, often as not,
She steps aside, I lose my thought—
And then I stumble,
Start to mumble,
Grumbling at the bumbling
Pilgrim that I am,
Skipping down life's winding path—
And then I laugh…!

"Keep trying," she says patiently,
"I will be with you presently."

Photography by Pam Boulding.

ISBN #978-1-934733-04-2 paperback
ISBN #978-1-934733-07-3 hardback

Poetry

Printed in the United States
200437BV00006B/1-210/A

9 781934 733042